Notebook of a Return to the Native Land

Wesleyan Poetry

AIMÉ CÉSAIRE

Notebook of a Return to the Native Land

TRANSLATED AND EDITED BY
CLAYTON ESHLEMAN AND
ANNETTE SMITH

Wesleyan University Press

Middletown, Connecticut

Published by Wesleyan University Press, Middletown, CT 06459

Front matter, translation, and critical apparatus ©2001 by Clayton Eshleman
and Annette Smith

Printed in the United States of America

5 4 3 2

CIP data appear at the end of the book

"Un grand poète noir" by André Breton © SNE Pauvert, 1979,
Librairie Arthème Fayard, 2000, was originally published as the
preface to the 1947 edition of *Cahier d'un retour au pays natal*.
It is used here by permission of Librairie Arthème Fayard.

An earlier version of this translation appeared in *Aimé Césaire: The Collected Poetry*
published by the University of California Press in 1984.

Contents

A Note on André Breton, by Annette Smith   vii

A Great Black Poet, by André Breton   ix

Notebook of a Return to the Native Land   1

Commentary   53

Notes   59

A Césaire Chronology   65

A Note on André Breton

Annette Smith

André Breton (1896–1966) is considered the figurehead of the French Surrealist movement, which was derived from the Zurich-based "Dada." Imported into France by the Rumanian Tristan Tzara, "Dada" represented a literary and artistic rebellion against the values of the contemporary world, and especially the bourgeois world. Surrealism anchored itself easily enough in France, a country already prepared for subversive writings by the works of such authors as Lautréamont, Rimbaud, Alfred Jarry, and Guillaume Apollinaire. Its principal tenet was its faith in a nonrational approach to reality, in the unconscious as revealed through dreams and automatic writing, and in the cultivation of the bizarre, the scandalous, and the iconoclastic.

The only unflinching Surrealist, in a group otherwise characterized by its fluidity, Breton became the theorist of the movement in several manifestos as well as in his novel *Nadja* (1928). During his stay in Paris, from 1932 to 1939, Césaire was, of course, exposed to a good deal of Surrealistic works, which happened to resonate both with his personal aesthetics and with the countercultural aesthetics and political goals of the budding Negritude movement (see p. 15). Shortly after the 1939 Paris publication of the *Notebook*, Césaire returned to a Martinique riddled not only with long-standing colonial problems, but with more immediate ones. For, after the defeat of France in 1940, the island passed under the control of the pro-Nazi Vichy government, whose distinctly anti-republican, censorious, and racist policies worsened the already grim situation of the black population of Martinique. It was to provide a dynamic response to this situation that in 1941 Césaire and other Martinican intellectuals founded the review *Tropiques*. This publication aimed at adapting the values of Surrealism to the specific context of Martinique, while exalting and exploring the concept of Negritude.

At this point, a felicitous conjunction took place: in April 1941, on his way to voluntary exile in the United States, André Breton made a stopover in Fort-de-France, stumbled upon the first issue of *Tropiques*, met Césaire and his friends, and subsequently read the *Notebook*. The following 1943 Breton essay we translate here, "Un Grand Poète noir," records this incandescent moment and was to serve as a preface to the 1947 first bilingual edition of the *Notebook*, which Breton godfathered from New York.

A Great Black Poet

André Breton

April 1941. Blocking the view, affixed to the beach by madre-
pores and visited by surf—at least the children had the play-
ground of their dreams to romp in all day long—a ship's carcass
in its very fixity provided no respite to the exasperating impos-
sibility of moving about other than with measured steps in the
space between two bayonets: the Lazaret concentration camp,
in the harbor of Fort-de-France. Released after a few days,
with what voracity did I plunge into the streets, seeking what-
ever still novel experience they could offer, dazzling markets,
the hummingbirds in voices, the women whom Paul Eluard
had described, upon returning from around the world, as more
beautiful than any others. Soon, however, another shipwreck
was looming, threatening to again block the entire horizon:
The city itself was adrift, deprived as it were of its essential
parts. Shops, and everything in their windows, took on a dis-
quieting, abstract character. Activity was a bit slower than need
be, noise too clear as if through beached debris. In the subtle air
the continuous ringing, far off, of an alarm bell.

It is under these circumstances that, apropos of buying a rib-
bon for my daughter, I happened to leaf through a periodical on

display in the haberdashery where the ribbon was sold. It was, under an extremely unpretentious cover, the first issue of a review called *Tropiques,* which had just come out in Fort-de-France. Needless to say, knowing the extent to which ideas had been debased in the last year and not unfamiliar with the lack of scruples characteristic of police reactions in Martinique, I approached this periodical with extreme diffidence . . . I could not believe my eyes: For what was said there was what had to be said and it was said in a manner not only as elegant but as elevated as anyone could say it! All the grimacing shadows were torn apart, scattered; all the lies, all the mockery shredded: Thus the voice of man was in no way broken, suppressed—it sprang upright again like the very spike of light. *Aimé Césaire,* such was the name of the one who spoke.

I shall not pretend that I did not at once take some pride in the fact that what he expressed was in no way unfamiliar; the names of the poets and authors he referred to would have been in themselves sufficient evidence; but even more the tone of those pages rang true, demonstrating that a man was totally engaged in an adventure while having at his command all that was required to establish something not only of an aesthetic but of a moral and social nature—or better, to make his intervention necessary and inevitable. The texts that accompanied Césaire's indicated persons with generally the same tendencies and whose thinking fully coincided with his own. In complete contrast to the writings with a masochistic, not to say servile, propensity that had been published in France in recent months,

Tropique persisted in opening up a royal road. "We belong," Césaire proclaimed, "to those who say *no* to darkness."

This land he was revealing and that his friends helped reconnoiter, it was my land too, yes, it was *our* land that I had wrongly feared obliterated by darkness. And one could feel that he was revolting and even before becoming more acquainted with his message, one noticed, so to speak, that from the simplest to the rarest, all the words processed by his tongue had been stripped, hence allowing that climax in concreteness, that unfailingly major quality of tone by which one can so easily tell the great poets from the lesser ones. What I learned that day was that the verbal instrument had not gotten out of tune in the tempest. This had to mean that the world was not in perdition: It would regain its soul.

By one of those flukes characteristic of the most auspicious moments, the West Indian haberdasher soon identified herself as the sister of René Ménil who was, along with Césaire, the main driving force behind *Tropiques*. Her mediation reduced to a minimum the conveying of the few words I scribbled in haste on her counter. Indeed, less than an hour later, after looking for me all over the streets, she gave me an appointment arranged by her brother. Menil: genuine culture in its least ostentatious form, impeccable restraint, but nevertheless nerve with all its tremoring currents.

And the next day, Césaire. I recall my first quite elementary reaction at finding him of a black so pure and even more unnoticeable at first because he was smiling. Through him (I already know it, I see it and everything will confirm it later), human essence is heated to a point of maximum effervescence in which knowledge—here of the highest order—overlaps with magical gifts. In my eyes his emergence, and I do not mean merely that day, in a form sheerly his own, takes on the value of a *sign of our times.* Thus, defying single-handedly an era in which we appear to be witnessing the general abdication of the mind, in which nothing appears to be created except for the purpose of perfecting the triumph of death, in which art itself threatens to congeal in obsolete schemes, the first revivifying new breath capable of restoring confidence comes from a black. And it is a black who handles the French language in a manner that no white man is capable of today. And it is a black who guides us today into the unexplored, establishing along the way, as if by child's play, the contacts that make us advance on sparks. And it is a black who is not only a black but *all* of man, who conveys all of man's questionings, all of his anguish, all of his hopes and all of his ecstasies and who will remain more and more for me the prototype of dignity.

Our meetings, in the evenings, after his high school classes (which were at that time focusing on Rimbaud) in a bar turned into a single crystal by the outside light, the gatherings on the terrace of his house made even more enchanting by the presence of Suzanne Césaire, who radiated like flambé punch, but even more an excursion into the heart of the island: I shall always see us, without any other landmark to navigate through an ocean of delirious vegetation than the large, enigmatic balisier flower,

which is a threefold heart throbbing on the tip of a spear, lean-
ing dangerously from very high over the abyss of Absalom as if
over the very crucible in which poetic images are transformed
when powerful enough to shake the world. It is there, under
the auspices of that flower, that this mission, assigned to man
today, of breaking violently with the modes of thinking and
feeling that eventually render his existence impossible took on
imprescriptable form. That once and for all I was confirmed in
the idea that nothing will do short of lifting a certain number of
taboos, of finally eliminating from human blood the deadly
toxins fostered in it by the (let's face it) lazier and lazier belief in
a beyond, the esprit de corps absurdly linked to nations and
races, and (supreme abjection) the power of money. Inevitably,
for the past century, it has devolved upon poets to split open
the armature that stifles us, and it is significant to note that
posterity tends to consecrate only those who have taken this
task the furthest.

That afternoon, facing the luxurious opening of all the flood-
gates of greenery, I truly valued a feeling of total communion
with one of them, of knowing him above all as a man of will and
of not distinguishing essentially his will from my own.

I also valued having solid evidence that he was a person of
total achievement: A few days earlier he had given me an off-
print of his *Notebook of a Return to the Native Land* from a small
Parisian journal in which the poem must have passed unnoticed
in 1939, and that poem is nothing less than the greatest lyrical
monument of our times. It brought me the rarest of certainties,

one that can never be attained by oneself: Its author had gambled on everything that I had ever believed in and he had, unquestionably, won. The stakes—taking into account Césaire's specific genius—were our common conception of life.

To begin with, one will find in his poetry that luxuriance of movement, that at times spurting, at times showering exuberance, that ability to constantly and deeply stir the affective world—all traits characteristic of authentic poetry in contrast to the fake poetry, poisonous would-be poetry, constantly proliferating around it. *To sing or not to sing,* that is the question and there is no salvation in poetry for someone who does not *sing,* although the poet is expected to do *more* than sing. And needless to say that when one who does not sing resorts to rhyme, fixed meter, and other bogus devices, he will only fool the ears of Midas. Aimé Césaire is first and foremost one who sings.

Once that first absolutely necessary but not sufficient condition is fulfilled, a poetry worthy of its name is measured by the degree of abstention, of *refusal,* it implies, and that negative component of its nature must be maintained as essential: It balks at tolerating anything already seen, heard, agreed upon, at using anything already used except when diverting it from its previous function. In this respect, Césaire is one of the most demanding poets not only because he is probity itself, but because of the extent of his culture, the quality and breadth of his knowledge.

Finally—and here, to remove any doubt brought about by the fact that, exceptionally, *Notebook of a Return to the Native Land* is a poem "with a theme," if not "a thesis," I specify that I am referring just as much to the poems of a different tenor that followed it—the value of Césaire's poetry, as with all great poetry and all great art, rests principally in the power of transmutation that it brings into play: namely, in turning the most discredited materials, including even ugliness and servitude, into not just gold or the philosophic stone but into freedom itself.[1]

The gift of song, the capacity for refusal, the power of extraordinary transmutation that I have just mentioned cannot be idly reduced to a handful of technical secrets. All that one can legitimately say is that all three find the largest common denominator in an exceptional and, until further notice, irreducible intensity of emotion confronting the spectacle of life (to the point where one is moved to change it). At most, critics are permitted to say something about the conflicting aspects of the formation of the personality in question and to bring out the striking circumstances of that formation. Unquestionably in Césaire's case, it would *for once* lead us, at full gallop, away from the path of indifference.

In this respect, *Notebook of a Return to the Native Land* is a unique, irreplaceable document. The very title, as understated as it is, aims at placing the reader at the core of a conflict that most affects the author, a conflict that he must, at all costs, transcend. The poem was written in Paris, after Césaire had just left the Ecole Normale Supérieure and was about to return to Martinique. His native land, yes, how could one resist the call of this particular island, who would not succumb to its skies, its siren-like beckonings, its language oh so cajoling? But in no time at all darkness encroaches: One need only put oneself in Césaire's place to understand what assaults this nostalgia must sustain. Behind this floral design there is the wretchedness of a colonized people, their shameless exploitation by a handful of parasites in defiance of the very laws of their mother country and without any qualms about dishonoring it; there is the resignation of this people, geographically disadvantaged by being a mere scattering of islands here and there. Behind all of this, only a few generations back, there is slavery and here the wound reopens, yawning with the entire width of a lost Africa,[2] with ancestral memories of abominable tortures, with the awareness of a monstrous and forever irreparable denial of justice inflicted upon an entire collectivity. A collectivity to which the returning poet belongs body and soul, as enriched as he may have been by all the teachings of the white world and thereby at that moment all the more torn.

Quite naturally the *Notebook* becomes an arena for revindication, bitterness, sometimes despair, to compete in, and the author opens himself up to the most dramatic taking stock. His revindication, one can never point out enough, is the most legitimate in the world, so much so that the merest consideration of justice should prompt the white to grant it. But we are still a long way from that, even if we are beginning to put it timidly on the agenda: "In the former colonies, which will fall under a new regime and whose evolution towards democracy will become an international issue, democracy will have to put an end not only to the exploitation of colored people but to the social and political 'racism' of the white man."[3] One awaits with equal impatience the day when, outside these colonies, the great mass of colored people will no longer be insultingly segregated and restricted to inferior jobs or worse. If this expectation is not met by the international settlements that will come into play at the end of the present war, one might be forced to endorse, once and for all and with all that it implies, the opinion that the emancipation of colored people can only be brought about by themselves.

However, as fundamental as Césaire's revindication appears to be, to limit its implications to the immediate would mean reducing its scope unforgivably. What I find invaluable in it is that it constantly transcends the anguish a black associates with the fate of black people in modern society, and that, becoming one with the anguish of all poets, artists, and bona fide thinkers, but adding to it the bonus of verbal genius, it encompasses the condition allotted to *man* by that society even to its unbearable, but also infinitely amendable, dimensions. And here comes to the fore in bold type what surrealism has always considered as the first article of its charter: a deliberate will to deal the coup de grâce to that which one calls "common sense" (which does not stop short of calling itself "reason"), and the imperious need to do away with the deadly division in the human spirit in which one component has managed to give itself complete license at the expense of the other, whereas the very suppression of the latter will inevitably end up exalting it. If slave traders have physically disappeared from the world stage, their vile spirit is undoubtedly still at work. For just as their "ebony wood" became this slap dash cargo, not even good enough to rot in the hold of their ships, so our dreams, that better half of our nature, become disenfranchised. "Because we hate you, you and your reason, we claim kinship with dementia praecox, with the flaming madness of persistent cannibalism . . . Put up with me, I won't put up with you." And suddenly this transfiguring gaze, a bluish fuzz on the embers as if the promise had been made of a redemption: Behold the one Césaire and I see as the greatest prophet of times to come, I mean Isidore Ducasse, Count of Lautréamont: *"Lautréamont's poetry, beautiful like a writ of expropriation* . . . Into lyrical and pallid strewings—like the fingers of the tropical pear tree when they fall in the gangrene of evening—he piles up the death trumpets of a laughable philosophy which raises to the dignity of wonder in a hierarchized world man, feet, hands and navel—a howling of fists against the barrier of the sky. . . . The first to have understood that poetry starts with excess, disproportion, quests deemed unacceptable, amidst the great blind tom-tom . . . up to the incomprehensible shower of stars."[4]

Aimé Césaire's voice, beautiful like nascent oxygen.

Tr. by Annette Smith and Clayton Eshleman

Notes

1. I did not wait to read this statement (published in *Lettres françaises* no. 7–8, 1943) in order to embrace its opposite: "I see poetry essentially as a form of writing which, in compliance not only with the rules of prose but with other rules specific to it, number, rhythm, regular assonance, must nevertheless surpass it in power. . . . Thus I demand that poetry possess all the qualities of prose, in the first place: nakedness, precision, clarity. . . . The poet must aim at expressing all and only what he has in mind. Ultimately nothing utterable, hinted at, no evocative images, no mystery." Roger Caillois, often better inspired, makes here a perfectly philistine statement.

2. Referring to the observations of European navigators at the end of the Middle Ages, Léo Frobenius writes: "When they arrived in the Bay of Guinea and landed at Vaida, the captains were surprised to find there well-designed streets, lined, for several miles, by double rows of trees; for many days they moved through a countryside covered with magnificent fields, populated by men clad in dazzling clothes of which they themselves had woven the fabric! Further south, in the kingdom of the Congo, a swarming crowd, dressed in 'silk' and 'velvet,' large states, well-organized down to the smallest detail, powerful sovereigns, prosperous industries. Civilized to the core!" (cited in *Tropiques* no. 5, 1942).

3. Pierre Cot: "The different kinds of democratic constitutions" (*Le Monde libre* no. 2, 1943).

4. Aimé Césaire: "Isidore Ducasse, Comte de Lautréamont" (*Tropiques* no. 6–7, 1943).

New York City, 1943

Notebook of a Return to the Native Land

At the end of daybreak . . .

Beat it, I said to him, you cop, you lousy pig, beat it, I detest the flunkies of order and the cockchafers of hope. Beat it, evil grigri, you bedbug of a petty monk. Then I turned toward paradises lost for him and his kin, calmer than the face of a woman telling lies, and there, rocked by the flux of a never exhausted thought I nourished the wind, I unlaced the monsters and heard rise, from the other side of disaster, a river of turtledoves and savanna clover which I carry forever in my depths height-deep as the twentieth floor of the most arrogant houses and as a guard against the putrefying force of crepuscular surroundings, surveyed night and day by a cursed venereal sun.

At the end of daybreak burgeoning with frail coves, the hungry Antilles, the Antilles pitted with smallpox, the Antilles dynamited by alcohol, stranded in the mud of this bay, in the dust of this town sinisterly stranded.

At the end of daybreak, the extreme, deceptive desolate eschar on the wound of the waters; the martyrs who do not bear

See the Notes section that follows the translation for commentary on words in lines marked by an asterisk.

witness; the flowers of blood that fade and scatter in the empty wind like the screeches of babbling parrots; an aged life mendaciously smiling, its lips opened by vacated agonies; an aged poverty rotting under the sun, silently; an aged silence bursting with tepid pustules,

the awful futility of our raison d'être.

At the end of daybreak, on this very fragile earth thickness exceeded in a humiliating way by its grandiose future—the volcanoes will explode,* the naked water will bear away the ripe sun stains and nothing will be left but a tepid bubbling pecked at by sea birds—the beach of dreams and the insane awakening.

At the end of daybreak, this town sprawled-flat, toppled from its common sense, inert, winded under its geometric weight of an eternally renewed cross, indocile to its fate, mute, vexed no matter what, incapable of growing with the juice of this earth, self-conscious, clipped, reduced, in breach of fauna and flora.

At the end of daybreak, this town sprawled-flat . . .

And in this inert town, this squalling throng so astonishingly detoured from its cry as this town has been from its movement, from its meaning, not even worried, detoured from its true cry, the only cry you would have wanted to hear because you feel it alone belongs to this town; because you feel it lives in it in some deep refuge and pride in this inert town, this throng detoured from its cry of hunger, of poverty, of revolt, of hatred, this throng so strangely chattering and mute.

In this inert town, this strange throng which does not pack, does not mix: clever at discovering the point of disencasement, of flight, of dodging. This throng which does not know how to throng, this throng, so perfectly alone under the sun, like a woman one thought completely occupied with her lyric cadence, who abruptly challenges a hypothetical rain and enjoins it not to fall; or like a rapid sign of the cross without perceptible motive; or like the sudden grave animality of a peasant, urinating standing, her legs parted, stiff.

In this inert town, this desolate throng under the sun, not connected with anything that is expressed, asserted, released in broad earth daylight, its own. Neither with Josephine, Empress of the French,* dreaming way up there above the nigger scum. Nor with the liberator fixed in his whitewashed stone liberation. Nor with the conquistador. Nor with this contempt, with this freedom, with this audacity.

At the end of daybreak, this inert town and its beyond of lepers, of consumption, of famines, of fears crouched in the ravines, fears perched in the trees, fears dug in the ground, fears adrift in the sky, of piled up fears and their fumaroles of anguish.

At the end of daybreak, the morne* forgotten, forgetful of leaping.

At the end of daybreak, the morne in restless, docile hooves —its malarial blood routs the sun with its overheated pulse.

At the end of daybreak, the restrained conflagration of the morne like a sob gagged on the verge of a bloodthirsty burst, in quest of an ignition that slips away and ignores itself.

At the end of daybreak, the morne crouching before bulimia on the outlook for tuns and mills, slowly vomiting out its human fatigue, the morne solitary and its shed blood, the morne bandaged in shade, the morne and its ditches of fear, the morne and its great hands of wind.

At the end of daybreak, the famished morne and no one knows better than this bastard morne why the suicide choked* with a little help from his hypoglossal jamming his tongue backward to swallow it, why a woman seems to float belly up on the Capot River* (her chiaroscuro body submissively organized at the command of her navel) but she is only a bundle of sonorous water.

And neither the teacher in his classroom, nor the priest at catechism will be able to get a word out of this sleepy little nigger, no matter how energetically they drum on his shorn skull, for starvation has quicksanded his voice into the swamp of hunger (a-word-one-single-word and we-will-forget-about-Queen-Blanche-of-Castille,* a-word-one-single-word, you-should-see-this-little-savage-who-doesn't-know-any-of-The-Ten-Commandments)

> for his voice gets lost in the swamp of hunger,
> and there is nothing, really nothing to squeeze out of this
>> little brat,
> other than a hunger which can no longer climb to the
>> rigging of his voice,
> a sluggish flabby hunger,
> a hunger buried in the depth of the Hunger of this
>> famished morne

At the end of daybreak, the disparate stranding, the exacerbated stench of corruption, the monstrous sodomies of the host and the sacrificing priest, the impassable beakhead frames of prejudice and stupidity, the prostitutions, the hypocrisies, the lubricities, the treasons, the lies, the frauds, the concussions—the panting of a deficient cowardice, the heave-holess enthusiasm of supernumerary sahibs, the greeds, the hysterias, the perversions, the clownings of poverty, the cripplings, the itchings, the hives, the tepid hammocks of degeneracy. Right here the parade of laughable and scrofulous buboes, the forced feedings of very strange microbes, the poisons without known alexins, the sanies of really ancient sores, the unforeseeable fermentations of putrescible species.

At the end of daybreak, the great motionless night, the stars deader than a caved-in balafon,

the teratical bulb of night, sprouted from our villainies and our self-denials.

And our foolish and crazy stunts to revive the golden splashing of privileged moments, the umbilical cord restored to its ephemeral splendor, the bread, and the wine of complicity, the bread, the wine, the blood of honest weddings.

And this joy of former times making me aware of my present poverty, a bumpy road plunging into a hollow where it scatters a few shacks; an indefatigable road charging at full speed a morne at the top of which it brutally quicksands into a pool of clumsy houses, a road foolishly climbing, recklessly descending, and the carcass of wood, which I call "our house," comically perched on minute cement paws, its coiffure of corrugated iron in the sun like a skin laid out to dry, the main room, the rough floor where the nail heads gleam, the beams of pine and shadow across the ceiling, the spectral straw chairs, the grey lamp light, the glossy flash of cockroaches in a maddening buzz . . .

At the end of daybreak, this most essential land restored to my gourmandise, not in diffuse tenderness, but the tormented sensual concentration of the fat tits of the mornes with an occasional palm tree as their hardened sprout, the jerky orgasm of torrents and from Trinité to Grand-Rivière,* the hysterical grandsuck of the sea.

And time passed quickly, very quickly.

After August and mango trees decked out in all their lunules, September begetter of cyclones, October igniter of sugarcane, November who purrs in the distilleries, there came Christmas.

It had come in first, Christmas did, with a tingling of desires, a thirst for new tenderness, a burgeoning of vague dreams, then with a purple rustle of its great joyous wings it had suddenly flown away, and then its abrupt fall out over the village that made the shack life burst like an overripe pomegranate.

Christmas was not like other holidays. It didn't like to gad about the streets, to dance on public squares, to mount the carousel horses, to use the crowd to pinch women, to hurl fireworks into the faces of the tamarind trees. It had agoraphobia, Christmas did. What it wanted was a whole day of bustling, preparing, a cooking and cleaning spree, endless jitters,

about-not-having-enough,

about-running-short,

about-getting-bored,

then at evening an unimposing little church, which would benevolently make room for the laughter, the whispers, the secrets, the love talk, the gossip and the guttural cacophony of a plucky singer and also boisterous pals and shameless hussies and shacks up to their guts in succulent goodies, and not stingy, and twenty people can crowd in, and the street is deserted, and the village turns into a bouquet of singing, and you are cozy in there, and you eat good, and you drink hearty and there are blood sausages, one kind only two fingers wide twined in coils, the other broad and stocky, the mild one tasting of wild thyme, the hot one spiced to an incandescence, and steaming coffee and sugared anise and milk punch, and the liquid sun of rums, and all sorts of good things which drive your taste buds wild or distill them to the point of ecstasy or cocoon them with fragrances, and you laugh, and you sing, and the refrains flare on and on like cocopalms:

Alleluia
Kyrie eleison . . . leison . . . leison,
Christe eleison . . . leison . . . leison.

And not only do the mouths sing, but the hands, the feet, the buttocks, the genitals, and your entire being liquefies into sounds, voices, and rhythm.

At the peak of its ascent, joy bursts like a cloud. The songs don't stop, but roll now anxious and heavy through the valleys of fear, the tunnels of anguish and the fires of hell.

And each one starts pulling the nearest devil by the tail, until fear imperceptibly fades in the fine sand lines of dream, and you really live as in a dream, and you drink and you shout and you sing as in a dream, and doze too as in a dream, with rose

petal eyelids, and the day comes velvety as a sapodilla, and the liquid manure smell of the cacao trees, and the turkeys shelling their red pustules in the sun, and the obsessive bells, and the rain,
the bells . . . the rain . . .
that tinkle, tinkle, tinkle . . .

At the end of daybreak, this town sprawled-flat . . .

It crawls on its hands without the slightest desire to drill the sky with a stature of protest. The backs of the houses are afraid of the sky truffled with fire, their feet of the drownings of the soil, they chose to perch shallowly between surprises and treacheries. And yet the town advances, yes it does. It even grazes every day further beyond its tide of tiled corridors, prudish shutters, gluey courtyards, dripping paintwork. And petty hushed-up scandals, petty unvoiced guilts, petty immense hatreds knead the narrow streets into bumps and potholes where the wastewater grins longitudinally through turds . . .

At the end of daybreak, life prostrate, you don't know how to dispose of your aborted dreams, the river of life desperately torpid in its bed, neither turgid nor low, hesitant to flow, pitifully empty, the impartial heaviness of boredom distributing shade equally on all things, the air stagnant, unbroken by the brightness of a single bird.

At the end of daybreak, another little house very bad-smelling in a very narrow street, a minuscule house which harbors in its guts of rotten wood dozens of rats and the turbulence of my six brothers and sisters, a cruel little house whose demands panic the ends of our months and my temperamental father gnawed by one persistent ache, I never knew which one, whom an unexpected sorcery could lull to melancholy tenderness or drive to towering flames of anger; and my mother whose legs pedal, pedal, night and day, for our tireless hunger, I was even awakened at night by these tireless legs which pedal the night and the bitter bite in the soft flesh of the night of a Singer that my mother pedals, pedals for our hunger and day and night.

At the end of daybreak, beyond my father, my mother, the shack chapped with blisters, like a peach tree afflicted with curl, and the thin roof patched with pieces of gasoline cans, which create swamps of rust in the stinking sordid gray straw pulp, and when the wind whistles, these odds and ends make a noise bizarre, first like the crackling of frying, then like a brand dropped into water the smoke of its twigs flying up. And the bed of boards from which my race arose, my whole entire race from this bed of boards, with its kerosene case paws, as if it had elephantiasis, that bed, and its kidskin, and its dry banana leaves, and its rags, yearning for a mattress, my grandmother's bed (above the bed, in a jar full of oil a dim light whose flame dances like a fat cockroach . . . on this jar in gold letters: MERCI).*

And this rue Paille,* this disgrace,

an appendage repulsive as the private parts of the village which extends right and left, along the colonial highway, the grey surge of its shingled roofs. Here there are only straw roofs, spray browned and wind plucked.

Everyone despises rue Paille. It's there that the village youth go astray. It's there especially that the sea pours forth its garbage, its dead cats and croaked dogs. For the street opens onto the beach, and the beach alone cannot satisfy the sea's foaming rage.

A blight this beach as well, with its piles of rotting muck, its furtive rumps relieving themselves, and the sand is black,* funereal, you've never seen a sand so black, and the scum glides over it yelping, and the sea pummels it like a boxer, or rather the sea is a huge dog licking and biting the shins of the beach, biting them so fiercely that it will end up devouring it, the beach and rue Paille along with it.

At the end of daybreak, the wind of long ago—of betrayed trusts, of uncertain evasive duty and that other dawn in Europe—arises . . .

To go away.
As there are hyena-men and panther-men, I would be a jew-man
a Kaffir-man
a Hindu-man-from-Calcutta
a Harlem-man-who-doesn't-vote

the famine-man, the insult-man, the torture-man you can grab anytime, beat up, kill—no joke, kill—without having to account to anyone, without having to make excuses to anyone
a jew-man
a pogrom-man
a puppy
a beggar

but *can* one kill Remorse, perfect as the stupefied face of an English lady discovering a Hottentot skull in her soup tureen?

I would rediscover the secret of great communications and great combustions. I would say storm. I would say river. I would say tornado. I would say leaf. I would say tree. I would be drenched by all rains, moistened by all dews. I would roll like frenetic blood on the slow current of the eye of words turned into mad horses into fresh children into clots into curfew into vestiges of temples into precious stones remote enough to discourage miners. Whoever would not understand me would not understand any better the roaring of a tiger.

And you ghosts rise blue from alchemy from a forest of hunted beasts of twisted machines of a jujube tree of rotten flesh of a basket of oysters of eyes of a network of straps in the beautiful sisal of human skin I would have words vast enough to contain you and you earth taut earth drunk
earth great vulva raised to the sun

earth great delirium of God's mentula*
savage earth arisen from the storerooms of the sea a clump of
Cecropia in your mouth
earth whose tempestuous face I can only compare to the virgin
and foolish forest which were it in my power I would show in
guise of a face to the undeciphering eyes of men
all I would need is a mouthful of jiculi* milk to discover in you
always as distant as a mirage—a thousand times more native
and made golden by a sun that no prism divides—the earth
where everything is free and fraternal, my earth

To go away. My heart was pounding with emphatic gene-
rosities. To go away . . . I would arrive sleek and young in this
land of mine and I would say to this land whose loam is part of
my flesh: "I have wandered for a long time and I am coming
back to the deserted hideousness of your sores."

I would go to this land of mine and I would say to it: "Em-
brace me without fear . . . And if all I can do is speak, it is for
you I shall speak."

And again I would say:
"My mouth shall be the mouth of those calamities that have
no mouth, my voice the freedom of those who break down in
the prison holes of despair."
And on the way I would say to myself:
"And above all, my body as well as my soul, beware of assum-
ing the sterile attitude of a spectator, for life is not a spectacle,

a sea of miseries is not a proscenium, a man screaming is not a dancing bear . . ."

And behold here I am!

Once again this life hobbling before me, what am I saying life, *this death*, this death without sense or pity, this death that so pathetically falls short of greatness, the dazzling pettiness of this death, this death hobbling from pettiness to pettiness; these shovelfuls of petty greeds over the conquistador; these shovelfuls of petty flunkies over the great savage; these shovelfuls of petty souls over the three-souled Carib, and all these deaths futile
absurdities under the splashing of my open conscience
tragic futilities lit up by this single noctiluca
and I alone, sudden stage of this daybreak
when the apocalypse of monsters cavorts then,
capsized, hushes
warm election of cinders, of ruins and collapses

—One more thing! only one, but please make it only one: I have no right to measure life by my sooty finger span; to reduce myself to this little ellipsoidal nothing trembling four fingers above the line,* I a man, to so overturn creation that I include myself between latitude and longitude!

At the end of daybreak,
the male thirst and the desire stubborn,

here I am, severed from the cool oases of brotherhood
this so modest nothing bristles with hard splinters
this too safe horizon is startled like a jailer.

Your last triumph, tenacious crow of Treason.

What is mine, these few thousand deathbearers who mill in the calabash of an island and mine too, the archipelago arched with an anguished desire to negate itself, as if from maternal anxiety to protect this impossibly delicate tenuity separating one America from another; and these loins which secrete for Europe the hearty liquor of a Gulf Stream, and one of the two slopes of incandescence between which the Equator tightrope-walks toward Africa. And my non-fence island, its brave audacity standing at the stern of this polynesia, before it, Guadeloupe, split in two down its dorsal line and equal in poverty to us, Haiti where negritude rose for the first time* and stated that it believed in its humanity and the funny little tail of Florida where the strangulation of a nigger is being completed, and Africa gigantically caterpillaring up to the Hispanic foot of Europe, its nakedness where death scythes widely.

And I say to myself Bordeaux and Nantes and Liverpool and New York and San Francisco*
not an inch of this world devoid of my fingerprint
and my calcaneus on the spines of skyscrapers and my filth in the glitter of gems!
Who can boast of being better off than I?

Virginia. Tennessee. Georgia. Alabama
Monstrous putrefaction of revolts
stymied,
marshes of putrid blood
trumpets absurdly muted
Land red, sanguineous, consanguineous land.

What is also mine: a little cell in the Jura,*
a little cell, the snow lines it with white bars
the snow is a jailer mounting guard before a prison

What is mine
a lone man imprisoned in whiteness
a lone man defying the white screams of white death
(TOUSSAINT, TOUSSAINT LOUVERTURE)
a man who mesmerizes the white sparrow hawk of white
death
a man alone in the sterile sea of white sand
a coon grown old standing up to the waters of the sky
Death traces a shining circle above this man
death stars softly above his head
death breathes, crazed, in the ripened cane field of his arms
death gallops in the prison like a white horse*
death gleams in the dark like the eyes of a cat
death hiccups like water under the Keys*
death is a struck bird
death wanes

death flickers
death is a very shy patyura*
death expires in a white pool of silence.

Swellings of night in the four corners of this daybreak
convulsions of congealed death
tenacious fate
screams erect from mute earth
the splendor of this blood will it not burst open?

At the end of daybreak this land without a stele, these paths without memory, these winds without a tablet.
So what?
We would tell. Would sing. Would howl.
Full voice, ample voice, you would be our wealth, our spear pointed.

Words?
Ah yes, words!
Reason, I crown you evening wind.
Your name voice of order?
To me the whip's corolla.*
Beauty I call you the false claim of the stone.
But ah! my raucous laughter
smuggled in
Ah! my saltpeter treasure!
Because we hate you and your reason, we claim kinship with

dementia praecox with the flaming madness of persistent
cannibalism

Treasure, let's count:
the madness that remembers
the madness that howls
the madness that sees
the madness that is unleashed

And you know the rest

That 2 and 2 are 5
that the forest miaows
that the tree plucks the maroons* from the fire
that the sky strokes its beard
etc., etc. . . .

Who and what are we? A most worthy question!

From staring too long at trees I have become a tree and my
long tree feet have dug in the ground large venom sacs high
cities of bone
from brooding too long on the Congo
I have become a Congo resounding with forests and rivers
where the whip cracks like a great banner
the banner of a prophet
where the water goes

likouala-likouala*
where the angerbolt hurls its greenish axe forcing the boars of
putrefaction to the lovely wild edge of the nostrils.

At the end of daybreak the sun which hacks and spits up its
lungs

At the end of daybreak
a slow gait of sand
a slow gait of gauze
a slow gait of corn kernels

At the end of daybreak
a full gallop of pollen
a full gallop of a slow gait of little girls
a full gallop of hummingbirds
a full gallop of daggers to stave in the earth's breast

customs angels mounting guard over prohibitions at the gates
of foam

I declare my crimes and that there is nothing to say in my
defense.
Dances. Idols. An apostate. I too

I have assassinated God with my laziness with my words with
my gestures with my obscene songs

I have worn parrot plumes musk cat skins
I have exhausted the missionaries' patience
insulted the benefactors of mankind.
Defied Tyre. Defied Sidon.
Worshipped the Zambèze.

The extent of my perversity overwhelms me!
But why impenetrable jungle are you still hiding the total zero
of my mendacity and from a self-conscious concern for nobility
not celebrating the horrible leap of my Pahouin ugliness?

voum rooh oh*
voum rooh oh
to charm the snakes to conjure the dead
voum rooh oh
to compel the rain to turn back the tidal waves
voum rooh oh
to keep the shade from moving
voum rooh oh
that my own skies may open

—me on a road, a child, chewing sugar cane root
—a dragged man on a bloodspattered road a rope around his
neck
—standing in the center of a huge circus, on my black
forehead a crown of daturas

voum rooh
to fly off
higher than quivering higher than the sorceresses toward the
other stars ferocious exultation of forests and mountains up-
rooted at the hour when no one expects it the islands linked for
a thousand years!

voum rooh oh
that the promised times may return
and the bird who knew my name
and the woman who had a thousand names
names of fountain sun and tears
and her hair of minnows
and her steps my climates
and her eyes my seasons
and the days without injury
and the nights without offense
and the stars my confidence
and the wind my accomplice

But who misleads my voice? who grates my voice? Stuffing my
throat with a thousand bamboo fangs. A thousand sea urchin
stakes. It is you dirty end of the world. Dirty end of daybreak.
It is you weight of the insult and a hundred years of whip
lashes. It is you one hundred years of my patience, one hun-
dred years of my effort simply to stay alive.
rooh oh

we sing of venomous flowers flaring in fury-filled prairies; the skies of love cut with bloodclots; the epileptic mornings; the white blaze of abyssal sands, the sinking of flotsam in nights electrified with feline smells.

What can I do?

One must begin somewhere.

Begin what?

The only thing in the world worth beginning:

The End of the world of course.

Torte*
oh torte of the terrifying autumn
where new steel and perennial concrete grow
torte oh torte
where the air rusts in great sheets
of evil glee
where sanious water scars the great solar cheeks
I hate you

one still sees madras rags around the loins of women rings in their ears smiles on their lips babies at their nipples, these for starters:

ENOUGH OF THIS OUTRAGE!

So here is the great challenge and the satanic
compulsion and the insolent
nostalgic drift of April moons,
of green fires, of yellow fevers!

Vainly in the tepidity of your throat you ripen for the twenti-
eth time the same indigent solace that we are mumblers of
words

Words? while we handle quarters of earth, while we wed delir-
ious continents, while we force steaming gates, words, ah yes,
words! but words of fresh blood, words that are tidal waves and
erysipelas and malarias and lava and brush fires, and blazes of
flesh, and blazes of cities . . .

Know this:
the only game I play is the millennium
the only game I play is the Great Fear*

Put up with me. I won't put up with you!

Sometimes you see me with a great display of brains, snap up a
cloud too red
or a caress of rain, or a prelude of wind, don't fool yourself:

I am forcing the vitelline membrane* that separates me from
myself

I am forcing the great waters which girdle me with blood

I and I alone choose a seat on the last train of the last surge of
the last tidal wave

I and I alone
make contact with the latest anguish
I and oh, only I
secure through a straw
the first drops of virginal milk!

And now a last boo:
to the sun (not strong enough to inebriate my very tough head)
to the mealy night with its golden hatchings of erratic
fireflies
to the shock of hair trembling at the very top of the cliff
where the wind leaps in bursts of salty cavalries
I clearly read in my pulse that for me exoticism is no
provender

Leaving Europe utterly twisted with screams
the silent currents of despair
leaving timid Europe which collects and proudly overrates
itself

I summon this egotism beautiful
and bold
and my ploughing reminds me of an implacable cutwater.

So much blood in my memory! In my memory are lagoons.
They are covered with death's-heads. They are not covered
with water lilies. In my memory are lagoons. No women's loin-
cloths spread out on their shores.
My memory is encircled with blood. My memory has a belt of
corpses!
and machine gun fire of rum barrels brilliantly sprinkling our
ignominious revolts, amorous glances swooning from having
swigged too much ferocious freedom

(niggers-are-all-alike, I-tell-you
vices-all-the-vices, believe-you-me
nigger-smell, that's-what-makes-cane-grow
remember-the-old-saying:
beat-a-nigger, and you feed him)

among "rocking chairs" contemplating the voluptuousness of
quirts*
I circle about, an unappeased filly

Or else quite simply as they like to think of us!
Cheerfully obscene, completely nuts about jazz to cover their
extreme boredom.

I can boogie-woogie, do the Lindy-hop and tap-dance.
And for a special treat the muting of our cries muffled with
wah-wah. Wait . . .
Everything is as it should be. My good angel grazes the neon.
I swallow batons. My dignity wallows in puke . . .

Sun, Angel Sun, curly Angel of the Sun
for a leap beyond the sweet and greenish treading of the
waters of abjection!

But I approached the wrong sorcerer. On this exorcised
earth, cast adrift from its precious malignant purpose, this voice
that cries, little by little hoarse, vainly, vainly hoarse,

and there remains only the accumulated droppings of our
lies—and they do not respond.

What madness to dream up a marvelous caper above the
baseness!
Oh yes the Whites are great warriors
hosannah to the master and to the nigger-gelder!
Victory! Victory, I tell you: the defeated are content!
Joyous stenches and songs of mud!

By a sudden and beneficent inner revolution, I now honor
my repugnant ugliness.

On Midsummer Day, as soon as the first shadows fall on the village of Gros-Morne, hundreds of horse dealers gather on rue "De Profundis,"*

a name at least honest enough to announce an onrush from the shoals of Death. And it truly is from Death, from its thousand petty local forms (cravings unsatisfied by Para grass and tipsy bondage to the distilleries) that the astonishing cavalry of impetuous nags surges unfenced toward the great-life. What a galloping! what neighing! what sincere urinating! what prodigious droppings! "a fine horse difficult to mount!"—"A proud mare sensitive to the spur!"—"A fearless foal superbly pasterned!"

And the shrewd fellow whose waistcoat displays a proud watch chain, palms off, instead of full udders, youthful mettle and genuine contours, either the systematic puffiness from obliging wasps, or the obscene stings from ginger, or the helpful distribution of several gallons of sugared water.

I refuse to pass off my puffiness for authentic glory.

And I laugh at my former childish fantasies.

No, we've never been Amazons of the king of Dahomey, nor princes of Ghana with eight hundred camels, nor wise men in Timbuktu under Askia the Great, nor the architects of Djenné, nor Madhis,* nor warriors. We don't feel under our armpit the itch of those who in the old days carried a lance. And since I have sworn to leave nothing out of our history (I who love nothing better than a sheep grazing his own afternoon shadow), I may as well confess that we were at all times pretty mediocre dishwashers, shoeblacks without ambition, at best conscientious sorcerers and the only unquestionable record that we broke was that of endurance under the chicote . . .*

And this land screamed for centuries that we are bestial brutes; that the human pulse stops at the gates of the barracoon; that we are walking compost hideously promising tender cane and silky cotton and they would brand us with redhot irons and we would sleep in our excrement and they would sell us on the town square and an ell of English cloth and salted meat from Ireland cost less than we did, and this land was calm, tranquil, repeating that the spirit of the Lord was in its acts.

We the vomit of slave ships
We the venery of the Calabars*
what? Plug up our ears?
We, so drunk on jeers and inhaled fog that we rode the roll to death!
Forgive us fraternal whirlwind!

I hear coming up from the hold the enchained curses, the gasps of the dying, the noise of someone thrown into the sea . . . the baying of a woman in labor . . . the scrape of fingernails seeking throats . . . the flouts of the whip . . . the seething of vermin amid the weariness . . .

Nothing could ever lift us toward a noble hopeless adventure.
So be it. So be it.
I am of no nationality recognized by the chancelleries.
I defy the craniometer. *Homo sum* etc.
Let them serve and betray and die
So be it. So be it. It was written in the shape of their pelvis.*

And I, and I,
I was singing the hard fist
You must know the extent of my cowardice.
One evening on the streetcar facing me, a nigger.

A nigger big as a pongo trying to make himself small on the street-car bench. He was trying to leave behind, on this grimy bench, his gigantic legs and his trembling famished boxer hands. And everything had left him, was leaving him. His nose which looked like a drifting peninsula and even his negritude discolored as a result of untiring tawing. And the tawer was Poverty. A big unexpected lop-eared bat whose claw marks in his face had scabbed over into crusty islands. Or rather, Poverty was, like a tireless worker, laboring on some hideous cartouche. One could easily see how that industrious and malevolent thumb had kneaded bumps into his brow, bored two bizarre parallel tunnels in his nose, overexaggerated his lips, and in a masterpiece of caricature, planed, polished and varnished the tiniest cutest little ear in all creation.

He was a gangly nigger without rhythm or measure.

A nigger whose eyes rolled a bloodshot weariness.

A shameless nigger and his toes sneered in a rather stinking way at the bottom of the yawning lair of his shoes.

Poverty, without any question, had knocked itself out to finish him off.

It had dug the socket, had painted it with a rouge of dust mixed with rheum.

It had stretched an empty space between the solid hinge of the jaw and bone of an old tarnished cheek. Had planted over it the small shiny stakes of a two- or three-day beard. Had panicked his heart, bent his back.

And the whole thing added up perfectly to a hideous nigger, a grouchy nigger, a melancholy nigger, a slouched nigger, his hands joined in prayer on a knobby stick. A nigger shrouded in an old threadbare coat. A comical and ugly nigger, with some women behind me sneering at him.

He was COMICAL AND UGLY,*

COMICAL AND UGLY for sure.

I displayed a big complicitous smile . . .

My cowardice rediscovered!

Hail to the three centuries which uphold my civil rights and my minimized blood.

My heroism, what a farce!

This town fits me to a t.

And my soul is lying down. Lying down like this town in its refuse and mud.

This town, my face of mud.

For my face I demand the vivid homage of spit! . . .

So, being what we are, ours the warrior thrust, the triumphant knee, the well-plowed plains of the future? Look, I'd rather admit to uninhibited ravings, my heart in my brain like a drunken knee.

My star now, the funereal menfenil.*

And on this former dream my cannibalistic cruelties:

(The bullets in the mouth thick saliva
our heart from daily lowness bursts
the continents break the fragile bond of isthmuses lands leap in accordance with the fatal division of rivers and the morne which for centuries kept its scream within itself,
it is its turn to draw and quarter the silence
and this people an ever-rebounding spirit
and our limbs vainly disjointed by the most refined tortures and life even more impetuously springing up from this compost—unexpected as a soursop amidst the decomposition of breadfruit!)

On this dream so old in me my cannibalistic cruelties:

I was hiding behind a stupid vanity destiny called me
I was hiding behind it and suddenly there was a man on the ground,
his feeble defenses scattered,
his sacred maxims trampled underfoot, his pedantic rhetoric

oozing air through each wound.
there is a man on the ground
and his soul is almost naked
and destiny triumphs in watching this soul which
defied its metamorphosis in the ancestral slough.

I say that this is right.
My back will victoriously exploit the chalaza* of fibers.
I will deck my natural obsequiousness with gratitude.
And the silver-braided bullshit of the postillion* of Havana,
lyrical baboon pimp for the glamour of slavery, will be more
than a match for my enthusiasm.

I say that this is right.
I live for the flattest part of my soul.
For the dullest part of my flesh!

   Tepid dawn of ancestral heat and fear I now tremble with the
collective trembling that our docile blood sings in the madrepore.

And these tadpoles hatched in me by my prodigious ancestry!
Those who invented neither powder nor compass
those who could harness neither steam nor electricity
those who explored neither the seas nor the sky
but who know in its most minute corners the land of suffering
those who have known voyages only through uprootings

those who have been lulled to sleep by so much kneeling
those whom they domesticated and Christianized
those whom they inoculated with degeneracy
tom-toms of empty hands
inane tom-toms of resounding sores
burlesque tom-toms of tabetic treason

Tepid dawn of ancestral heat and fears
overboard with alien riches
overboard with my genuine falsehoods

But what strange pride suddenly illuminates me?

let the hummingbird come
let the sparrow hawk come
the breach in the horizon
the cynocephalus
let the lotus bearer of the world come
the pearly upheaval of dolphins cracking the shell of the sea
let a plunge of islands come
the disappearing of days of dead flesh in the quicklime of birds
of prey
let the ovaries of the water come where the future stirs its testicles
let the wolves come who feed in the untamed openings of the
body at the hour when my moon and your sun meet at the
ecliptic inn

under the reserve of my uvula there is a wallow of boars
under the gray stone of the day there are your eyes which are a
shimmering conglomerate of coccinella

in the glance of disorder there is this swallow of mint and
broom which melts always to be reborn in the tidal wave of
your light
(Calm and lull oh my voice the child who does not know that
the map of spring is always to be drawn again)

The tall grass will sway gentle ship of hope for the cattle
the long alcoholic sweep of the swell
the stars with the bezels of their rings never in sight
will cut the pipes of the glass organ of evening
zinnias
coryanthas will then be poured into the rich extremity of my
fatigue and you star please from your luminous foundation
draw lemurian being—of man's unfathomable sperm the yet
undared form
carried like an ore in woman's trembling belly!

oh friendly light
oh fresh source of light
those who invented neither powder nor compass
those who could harness neither steam nor electricity
those who explored neither the seas nor the sky
but those without whom the earth would not be the earth

gibbosity all the more beneficent as the bare earth
even more earth
silo where that which is earthiest about earth ferments and
ripens

My negritude is not a stone, its deafness hurled against
the clamor of the day
my negritude is not a leukoma of dead liquid over the earth's
dead eye
my negritude is neither tower nor cathedral
it takes root in the red flesh of the soil
it takes root in the ardent flesh of the sky
it breaks through opaque prostration with its upright patience.

Eia for the royal Cailcedra!*
Eia for those who never invented anything
for those who never explored anything
for those who never conquered anything
but yield, captivated, to the essence of things
ignorant of surfaces but captivated by the motion of all things
indifferent to conquering, but playing the game of the world

truly the eldest sons of the world
porous to all the breathing of the world
fraternal locus for all the breathing of the world
drainless channel for all the water of the world
spark of the sacred fire of the world

flesh of the world's flesh pulsating with the very motion of the world!

Tepid dawn of ancestral virtues

Blood! Blood! all our blood aroused by the male heart of the sun
those who know about the femininity of the moon's oily body
the reconciled exultation of antelope and star
those whose survival travels in the germination of grass!
Eia perfect circle of the world, enclosed concordance!

Hear the white world
horribly weary from its immense efforts
its stiff joints crack under the hard stars
its blue steel rigidities pierce the mystic flesh
hear its deceptive victories tout its defeats
hear the grandiose alibis of its pitiful stumbling

Pity for our omniscient and naive conquerors!

Eia for those who never invented anything
for those who never explored anything
for those who never conquered anything

Eia for joy
Eia for love

Eia for grief and its udders of reincarnated tears.

and here at the end of this daybreak my virile prayer
that I hear neither the laughter nor the screams, my eyes
fixed on this town which I prophesy, beautiful,
grant me the savage faith of the sorcerer
grant my hands the power to mold
grant my soul the sword's temper
I won't flinch. Make my head into a figurehead
and as for me, my heart, do not make me into a father nor a
brother
nor a son, but into the father, the brother, the son,
nor a husband, but the lover of this unique people.

Make me resist any vanity, but espouse its genius
as the fist the extended arm!
Make me a steward of its blood
make me a trustee of its resentment
make me into a man for the ending
make me into a man for the beginning
make me into a man of meditation
but also make me into a man of germination

make me into the executor of these lofty works
the time has come to gird one's loins like a brave man—*

But in doing so, my heart, preserve me from all hatred

do not make me into that man of hatred for whom I feel only
hatred
for entrenched as I am in this unique race
you still know my tyrannical love
you know that it is not from hatred of other races
that I demand of myself to become a hoer for this unique race
that what I want
is for universal hunger
for universal thirst

to summon it to generate,
free at last, from its intimate closeness
the succulence of fruit.

And be the tree of our hands!
it turns, for all, the wounds cut
in its trunk*
the soil works for all
and toward the branches a headiness of fragrant precipitation!

But before reaching the shores of future orchards
grant that I deserve those on their belt of sea
grant me my heart while awaiting the earth
grant me on the ocean sterile
but somewhere caressed by the promise of the clew-line
grant me on this diverse ocean
the obstinacy of the fierce pirogue
and its marine vigor.

See it advance rising and falling on the pulverized wave
see it dance the sacred dance before the grayness of the village
see it trumpet from a vertiginous conch
see the conch gallop up to the uncertainty of the mornes

and see twenty times over the paddles vigorously plow the
water
the pirogue rears under the attack of the swells, deviates for an
instant,
tries to escape, but the paddle's rough caress turns it,
then it charges, a shudder runs along the wave's spine,
the sea slobbers and rumbles
the pirogue like a sleigh glides onto the sand.

At the end of this daybreak, my virile prayer:
grant me pirogue muscles on this raging sea
and the irresistible gaiety of the conch of good tidings!

Look, now I am only a man, no degradation, no spit perturbs
him,
now I am only a man who accepts emptied of anger
(nothing left in his heart but immense love, which burns)

I accept . . . I accept . . . totally, without reservation . . .
my race that no ablution of hyssop mixed with lilies could purify
my race pitted with blemishes
my race ripe grapes for drunken feet

my queen of spittle and leprosy
my queen of whips and scrofula
my queen of squamae and chloasma
(oh those queens I once loved in the remote gardens of spring
against the illumination of all the candles of the chestnut trees!)*
I accept. I accept.
and the flogged nigger saying "Forgive me master"
and the twenty-nine legal blows of the whip*
and the four foot high cell
and the spiked carcan
and the hamstringing of my runaway audacity
and the fleur de lys flowing* from the red iron into the fat of
my shoulder
and Monsieur Vaultier Mayencourt's* dog house where I
barked six poodle months
and Monsieur Brafin
and Monsieur Fourniol
and Monsieur de la Mahaudière
and the yaws
the mastiff
the suicide
the promiscuity
the bootikin
the shackles
the rack
the cippus
the head screw

Look, am I humble enough? Have I enough calluses on my knees? Muscles on my loins?

Grovel in the mud. Brace yourself in the thick of the mud. Carry.

Earth of mud. Horizon of mud. Sky of mud. Dead of the mud, oh names to thaw in the palm of a feverish breathing!

Siméon Piquine, who never knew his father or mother, unheard of in any town hall and who wandered his entire life—searching for his name

Grandvorka—of him I only know that he died, crushed one harvest evening, it was his job, apparently, to throw sand under the wheels of the running locomotive, to help it across bad spots.

Michel who used to write me signing a strange name. Unlucky Michel address *Condemned District* and you their living brothers

Exélie Vêté Congolo Lemké Boussolongo what healer with his thick lips would suck from the depths of the gaping wound the tenacious secret of venom?

what cautious sorcerer would undo from your ankles the viscous tepidity of mortal rings?

Presences it is not on your back that I will make peace with the world.

Islands scars of the water
Islands evidence of wounds
Islands crumbs
Islands unformed

Islands cheap paper shredded upon the water
Islands stumps skewered side by side on the flaming sword of
the Sun

Mulish reason you will not stop me from casting on the waters
at the mercy of the currents of my thirst
your form, deformed islands,
your end, my defiance.

Annulose islands, single beautiful hull

And I caress you with my oceanic hands. And I turn you
around with the tradewinds of my speech. And I lick you with
my seaweed tongues.
And I sail you unfreebootable

Oh death your mushy marsh!
Shipwreck your hellish debris! I accept!

At the end of daybreak, lost puddles, wandering scents, beached hurricanes, demasted hulls, old sores, rotted bones, vapors, shackled volcanoes, shallow-rooted dead, bitter cry. I accept!

And my special geography too; the world map made for my own use, not tinted with the arbitrary colors of scholars, but with the geometry of my spilled blood, I accept

and the determination of my biology, not a prisoner to a facial angle, to a type of hair, to a well-flattened nose, to a clearly Melanian coloring, and negritude, no longer a cephalic index, or plasma, or soma, but measured by the compass of suffering

and the Negro every day more base, more cowardly, more sterile, less profound, more spilled out of himself, more separated from himself, more wily with himself, less immediate to himself,

I accept, I accept it all

and far from the palatial sea that foams beneath the suppurating syzygy of blisters, miraculously lying in the despair of my arms the body of my country, its bones shocked and, in its veins, the blood hesitating like a drop of vegetal milk at the injured point of a bulb . . .

Suddenly now strength and life assail me like a bull and the water of life overwhelms the papilla of the morne, now all the veins and veinlets are bustling with new blood and the enormous breathing lung of cyclones and the fire hoarded in volcanoes and the gigantic seismic pulse which now beats the measure of a living body in my firm conflagration.

And we are standing now, my country and I, hair in the wind, my hand puny in its enormous fist and now the strength is not in us but above us, in a voice that drills the night and the hearing like the penetrance of an apocalyptic wasp.* And the voice complains that for centuries Europe has force-fed us with lies and bloated us with pestilence,

for it is not true that the work of man is done
that we have no business being on earth
that we parasite the world
that it is enough for us to heel to the world whereas the work of man has only begun
and man still must overcome all the interdictions wedged in the recesses of his fervor
and no race has a monopoly on beauty, on intelligence, on strength
and there is room for everyone at the convocation of conquest
and we know now that the sun turns around our earth lighting the parcel designated by our will alone and that every star falls from sky to earth at our omnipotent command.

I now see the meaning of this trial by the sword: my country is the "lance of night" of my Bambara ancestors.* It shrivels and its point desperately retreats toward the haft when it is sprinkled with chicken blood and it says that its nature requires the blood of man, his fat, his liver, his heart, not chicken blood.

And I seek for my country not date hearts, but men's hearts which in order to enter the silver cities through the great trapezoidal gate, beat with warrior blood, and as my eyes sweep my kilometers of paternal earth I number its sores almost joyfully and I pile one on top of another like rare species, and my total is ever lengthened by unexpected mintings of baseness.

And there are those who will never get over not being made in the likeness of God but of the devil, those who believe that being a nigger is like being a second-class clerk; waiting for a better deal and upward mobility; those who beat the drum of compromise in front of themselves, those who live in their own oubliette; those who say to Europe: "You see, I *can* bow and scrape, like you I pay my respects, in short I am not different from you; pay no attention to my black skin: the sun did it."*

And there is the nigger pimp, the nigger askari, and all the zebras shaking themselves in various ways to get rid of their stripes in a dew of fresh milk.

And in the midst of all of that I say: right on! my grandfather dies, I say right on!
the old negritude progressively cadavers itself.

No bones about it: he was a good nigger.

The Whites say he was a good nigger, a really good nigger, massa's good ole darky.

I say right on!

He was a good nigger indeed,

poverty had wounded his chest and back and they had stuffed into his poor brain that a fatality impossible to trap weighed on him; that he had no control over his own fate; that an evil Lord had for all eternity inscribed Thou Shall Not in his pelvic constitution; that he must be a good nigger; must sincerely believe in his worthlessness, without any perverse curiosity to check out the fatidic hieroglyphs.

He was a very good nigger

and it never occurred to him that he could hoe, burrow, cut anything, anything else really than insipid cane

He was a very good nigger

And they threw stones at him, chunks of scrap iron, broken bottles, but neither these stones, nor this scrap iron, nor these bottles . . .

O peaceful years of God on this terraqueous clod!

and the whip argued with the bombilation of the flies over the sugary dew of our sores.

I say right on! The old negritude
progressively cadavers itself
the horizon breaks, recoils and expands
and through the shredding of clouds the flashing of a sign
the slave ship cracks everywhere . . . Its belly convulses and
resounds . . . The ghastly tapeworm of its cargo gnaws the
fetid guts of the strange suckling of the sea!
And neither the joy of sails filled like a pocket stuffed with
doubloons, nor the tricks played on the dangerous stupidity of
the frigates of order prevent it from hearing the threat of its in-
testinal rumblings

In vain to ignore them the captain hangs the biggest loud-
mouth nigger from the main yard or throws him into the sea,
or feeds him to his mastiffs

Reeking of fried onions the nigger scum rediscovers the bitter
taste of freedom in its spilled blood

And the nigger scum is on its feet

the seated nigger scum
unexpectedly standing
standing in the hold
standing in the cabins
standing on the deck
standing in the wind

standing under the sun
standing in the blood
   standing
     and
       free
standing and no longer a poor madwoman in its maritime
freedom and destitution gyrating in perfect drift
and there it is:
most unexpectedly standing
standing in the rigging
standing at the tiller
standing at the compass
standing at the map
standing under the stars

   standing
     and
       free

and the lustral ship fearlessly advances on the crumbling water.
And now our ignominious plops are rotting away!

by the clinking noon sea
by the burgeoning midnight sun
listen sparrow hawk that holds the keys to the orient
by the disarmed day
by the stony spurt of the rain
listen dogfish that watches over the occident

listen white dog of the north, black serpent of the south

that cinches the sky girdle

There still remains one sea to cross

oh still one sea to cross

that I may invent my lungs

that the prince may hold his tongue

that the queen may lay me

still one old man to murder

one madman to deliver

that my soul may shine bark shine

bark bark bark

and the owl my beautiful inquisitive angel may hoot.

The master of laughter?

The master of ominous silence?

The master of hope and despair?

The master of laziness? Master of the dance?

    It is I!

and for this reason, Lord,

the frail-necked men

receive and perceive deadly triangular calm

Rally to my side my dances

you bad nigger dances

to my side my dances

the carcan-cracker dance

the prison-break dance
the it-is-beautiful-good-and-legitimate-to-be-a-nigger-dance
Rally to my side my dances and let the sun bounce on the
racket of my hands
but no the unequal sun is not enough for me
coil, wind, around my new growth
light on my cadenced fingers
to you I surrender my conscience and its fleshy rhythm
to you I surrender the fire in which my weakness smolders
to you I surrender the "chain-gang"
to you the swamps
to you the non-tourist of the triangular circuit
devour wind
to you I surrender my abrupt words
devour and encoil yourself
and self-encoiling embrace me with a more ample shudder
embrace me unto furious us
embrace, embrace us
but having also bitten us
to the blood of our blood bitten us!
embrace, my purity mingles only with yours
so then embrace
like a field of even filaos
at dusk
our multicolored purities
and bind, bind me without remorse
bind me with your vast arms of luminous clay

bind my black vibration to the very navel of the world
bind, bind me, bitter brotherhood
then, strangling me with your lasso of stars
rise, Dove
rise
rise
rise
I follow you who are imprinted on my ancestral white cornea.
rise sky licker
and the great black hole where a moon ago I wanted to drown
it is there I will now fish the malevolent tongue of the night in
its motionless veerition!*

Commentary

The publishing history of this poem is as follows:

It first appeared in the Parisian periodical *Volontés* no. 20, 1939.

The first publication in book form was in *Cahier d'un retour au pays natal: Memorandum on my Martinique,* preface by A. Breton, trans. L. Abel and Y. Goll (New York: Brentano's, 1947).

The first French edition in book form was published under the title *Cahier d'un retour au pays natal* (Paris: Bordas, 1947), with the Breton preface.

Subsequent editions were published by Présence Africaine (Paris, 1956, 1960, and 1971). The 1971 edition was bilingual, with Césaire's text and Breton's preface/essay translated by E. Snyder.

In addition to France and the United States, editions exist in Great Britain (Penguin Books), Germany, Italy, Mexico, and Cuba.

Our translation first appeared in *Montemora* no. 6, 1978. It has been reprinted in *Aimé Césaire: The Collected Poetry* (Berkeley/Los Angeles: University of California Press, 1983); in *Conductors of the Pit: Major Works by Rimbaud, Vallejo, Césaire, Artaud, and Holan,* trans./co-trans. and ed. Clayton Eshleman (New York: Paragon House, 1988); and in *The Norton Anthology/World Masterpieces,* vol. 2 (New York: Norton, 1996).

* * *

The present translation is a revision of our 1983 one, which was based on the French text in Vol. 1 of Césaire's *Oeuvres complètes,* ed. by Jean-Paul Césaire (Fort-de-France, Martinique: Editions Desormeaux, 1976). It turns out that this 1976 text of the poem has a number of misprints that we reproduced in our 1983 translation, in particular line breaks and stanza endings.

In 1994, the Nigerian scholar Abiola Irele published a version of the poem (in French only) in *Aimé Césaire: Cahier d'un retour au pays natal,* with Introduction, Commentary, and Notes (in English) (Ibadan: New Horn Press Limited). Irele's version takes into consideration textual differences to be found in a 1962 bilingual German edition of the poem, which according to Irele Césaire himself approved. Then in 1994, Editions du Seuil (Paris) published *Aimé Césaire: La Poésie* (ed. by Daniel Maximin and Gilles Carpentier), in which the text for the *Cahier* differs slightly from Irele's version. In 2000, Ohio State University Press published Irele's *Cahier* edition.

Our revision here takes into consideration both the Irele and the Maximin/Carpentier formats (for which the wording is the same), but is not exactly like either, in regard to stanza breaks and line endings.

Notebook of a Return to the Native Land does not fall into any formal category. In spite of the amount of reflective prose poetry in it, it is more of an extended lyric or serial work than a narrative poem. And yet, in spite of its brevity epic-wise, it also has an epic sweep and a heroic narrator who struggles to affirm his race identification and destiny through a series of complex interactions between a self-in-formation and his colonized country. We should also keep in mind that the poet called this poem a "notebook," suggesting that it was notes of some sort as preparation for another finished work. Since Césaire went ahead to dedicate the rest of his life to nearly full-time political action, it is possible to read the *Notebook* as a vision to be grounded in a politically committed life. However, the poem also feels notational: in spite of its verve and coherence, there occurs erratic nongrammatical punctuation as well as eruptions of poetry into prose and vice versa—elements that have probably contributed to the problems involved in establishing a definitive text.

So while the poem is nonnarrative at large, the shifts in direction and highly emotional interjections act as constant transitions between cinematic overviews (such as the one that opens the poem), narratives, chants, and lists. Whenever a pattern of procedure presents itself, the writing immediately shifts gears. The *Notebook,* thus, is always in veer, always rounding a corner. On one hand, we somewhat know what to expect as readers, given the poem's unwavering political context. On the other hand, Césaire's inventiveness and "black humor" keep the writing from becoming predictable or agenda laden. In terms of its resounding weight relative to its casual-sounding title, *Notebook of a Return to the Native Land* may remind some readers of Wallace Stevens's "Notes Toward a Supreme Fiction."

The poem opens, after the initial burst (which contains all of Césaire's lifelong themes in nucleus), with a brooding, static overview of the psychic and geographical topology of Martinique, based on Basse-Pointe, where the poet was born. These strophes often evoke Lautréamont's *Maldoror*. A second movement is implied with the speaker's declaration of his urge to go away; suddenly the supine present is sucked into a whirlpool of abuses and horrors suffered by blacks throughout their colonized and present history. The nonnarrative, exploding juxtapositions reveal Césaire's commitment to surrealism, even though thematic development is constantly taking place. The second movement reaches its nadir in the passage where the speaker discovers himself mocking an utterly degraded black on a streetcar. The final, rushing third movement is ignited by the line: "But what strange pride suddenly illuminates me?" In a series of dialectical shifts between the emergence of a future hero who gives new life to the world and images from the slaves' "middle passage" of the past, the "sprawled-flat" passivity of the first movement is transformed into a standing insurrection on the slave ship and finally whirls up into the stars. The incredible burden of the poem is that of a parthenogenesis in which Césaire must conceive and give birth to himself while exorcising his introjected and collective white image of the black.

In our attempt to maintain Césaire's usual preference for family and genus classifications for botanical words in our translation, we have been helped by Elodie Jourdain's *Le vocabulaire*

du parler Créole de la Martinique (Paris: Klincksieck, 1956),
R. Pichon's *Quelques aspects de la nature aux Antilles* (Fort-de-
France, Martinique, 1967), and Lafcadio Hearn's *Two Years in
the French West Indies* (New York: Harpers, 1890).
Césaire's fascination with Caribbean fauna and flora possibly
began when his high school geography teacher took the stu-
dents out on field trips at a time when standard examination
questions in Martinique were based on mainland French his-
tory and geography. In a 1960 interview, Césaire declared:

> I am an Antillean. I want a poetry that is concrete, very Antillean, Mar-
> tinican. I must name Martinican things, must call them by their names. The
> cañafistula mentioned in the poem "Spirals" is a tree; it is also called the
> drumstick tree. It has large yellow leaves and its fruit are those big purplish
> bluish black pods, used also here as a purgative. The balisier resembles a
> plantain, but it has a red heart, a red florescence at its center which is really
> shaped like a heart. The cecropias are shaped like silver hands, yes, like the
> interior of a black's hand. All of these astonishing words are absolutely nec-
> essary, they are never gratuitous. (Thomas A. Hale, *Les Ecrits d'Aimé Cé-
> saire, Bibliographie Commentée* [Montréal: Les Presses de l'Université de
> Montréal, 1978], p. 406)

One can see, in the *Notebook,* how Césaire's adherence to
specific fauna and flora has been extended to historical and my-
thological aspects of slavery, including exact identifications of
whips, torture, and humiliation.
We have worked hard in our translation not to simplify
Césaire's vocabulary nor to offer explanations instead of pre-
cise translations. Besides using the lexicons already mentioned

(along with various encyclopedias, dictionaries of several languages—including African and Créole—botanical indexes, atlases, and history texts), one or both of us met with Césaire himself several times in Paris, always with a word list, which he went over carefully, sometimes checking a word in an African language dictionary that he had apparently not consulted for years. In the notes that follow, we have mainly commented on words and phrases whose historical or symbolical significance may not be familiar to readers. We have refrained from defining rare or technical words that can be found in international English dictionaries. For a stanza-by-stanza interpretation of the *Notebook,* we refer the reader to the previously mentioned book edited by Abiola Irele.

Notes

[Page 2]: *the volcanoes will explode:* a reference to Mount Pelée, which erupted in 1902, destroying Saint Pierre, the former capital of Martinique.

[Page 3]: *Josephine . . . conquistador:* Josephine Tascher de la Pagerie (1763–1814), the first wife of Napoléon Bonaparte. She was born in Martinique into the white settler class; she became "Empress of the French" when Napoléon took the title of "Emperor of the French" in 1804. The liberator is Victor Schoelcher (1804–1893), the French abolitionist whose statue stands in the present-day capital, Fort-de-France. The conquistador refers to Pierre Bélain d'Esnambuc, who occupied Martinique in 1635 and claimed it for France.

[Page 4]: *morne:* This term, "used through the French West Indies to designate certain altitudes (usually with beautiful and curious forms) of volcanic origin, is justly applied to the majority of Martinican hills, and unjustly sometimes to its mightiest elevation—Mount Pelée" (Hearn, *Two Years*). In Césaire's time, slum areas were often located on mornes on the outskirts of Martinican towns.

[Page 4]: *why the suicide choked:* Slaves committed suicide by choking on their own tongues (the hypoglossal nerves are at the base of the tongue).

[Page 4]: *the Capot River:* a stream in northern Martinique.

[Page 5]: *Queen-Blanche-of-Castille:* A French queen in the Middle Ages, mother of Saint Louis.

[Page 7]: *Trinité to Grand-Rivière:* towns in northern Martinique.

[Page 10]: *MERCI:* "thank you" (French); the inscription is probably addressed to God.

[Page 10]: *rue Paille:* "Straw Street" (French), a street in the poorest sections of Martinican towns, whose houses are roofed with straw.

[Page 11]: *the sand is black:* because of its volcanic origin.

[Page 13]: *mentula:* "penis" (Latin), based on an Indo-European stem designating a stick agitated to produce fire.

[Page 13]: *jiculi:* according to Césaire, a variation on the word "jiquilite," a kind of indigo tree planted in El Salvador in the 19th century. The word could also be a variation on "jiqui," a Cuban timber tree. Whatever it is, in the poem it suggests that its ingestion produces a hallucinatory effect.

[Page 14]: *little ellipsoidal nothing trembling four fingers above the line:* probably refers to Martinique, which is oval shaped and close to the equator. [Page 15]: *Haiti where negritude rose for the first time:* The Haitian slave revolt, led by Toussaint Louverture (1743–1803), brought about the independence of Haiti in 1804.

Although Césaire was by no means the sole exponent of negritude, the word is now inseparable from his name, and partially responsible for his prominent position in the Third World. Coined with his friends Léon-Gontran Damas and Léopold Senghor while editing their newspaper, *L'Etudiant noir* (The Black Student), in Paris in the mid-1930s, the word first appeared in poetry in the *Notebook*. A neologism, it is made up (perhaps on the model of the South American *negrismo*) by latinizing the derogatory word for a black ("nègre") and adding a suffix for abstract nouns (latitude, solitude, exactitude, etc.). It signified a response to the centuries-old problem of the alienated position of the blacks in history, and implicitly called upon blacks to reject assimilation and cultivate consciousness of their own racial qualities and heritage. For Césaire, identity in suffering, not genetic material, determined the bond among black people of different origins.

To consider negritude also brings up the problems in translating the word "nègre" when it occurs in the *Notebook*. Put briefly, the lexical background is as follows: Before the Second World War the French had three words to designate individuals or things belonging to the black race. The most euphemistic was "Noir" (noun or adjective). The derogatory was "négro." In between, on a sort of neutral and objective ground, was the word "nègre," used both as a noun or as an adjective (as in "l'art nègre"). For the general public, "noir" and "nègre" may very well have been interchangeable, but the very civilized and very complexed Antilleans considered themselves as "Noirs," the "nègres" being on that distant continent, Africa. And it is in this light that one must read Césaire's use of the word "nègre" and its derivatives, "négritude," "négrillon," and "négraille": he was making up a family of words based on what he considered to be the most insulting way to refer to a black. The paradox, of course, was that this implicit reckoning with the black's ignominy, this process of self-irony and self-denigration, was the necessary step on a path to a new self-image and spiritual rebirth. From the point of view of the translator, it is therefore important to translate "nègre" as "nigger" and its derivatives as derivatives or compounds of "nègre" and "nigger" (negritude, little nigger, and nigger scum).

[Page 15]: *Bordeaux . . . San Francisco:* Bordeaux and Nantes in France and

Liverpool in England were the principal ports from which, in a triangular circuit, the slave ships sailed out to Africa and, after being loaded with their human cargo, crossed to America, returning with produce to Europe. New York and San Francisco appear here as symbolic of the economic exploitation of black people.

[Page 16]: *the Jura:* Louverture was a self-educated slave who, by 1801, was governing the entire island of Haiti. A year later, he was seized by Napoléon-sent forces and returned to France, where he died in a dungeon at Fort-de-Joux in the French Jura.

[Page 16]: *a white horse:* probably, in this context, refers to Baron Samedi, the spirit of death in Haitian folk belief (comparable to the horse of death in European iconography).

[Page 16]: *the Keys:* coral reefs in the Caribbean.

[Page 17]: *patyura:* according to Césaire, a variation on "patira," the name of a peccary found in Paraguay.

[Page 17]: *corolla:* the strands of a whip used on slaves.

[Page 18]: *maroons* from the French "marron," a chestnut, or, as an adjective, chestnut-colored. The secondary meaning in the West Indies (perhaps influenced by the American Spanish "cimarron"—wild, unruly, or runaway) applies to a black fugitive slave, or his black descendant. Runaway slaves, hiding in trees, often made animal sounds as signals to each other. Césaire's ironic use of the phrase is derived from a popular French saying, "tirer les marrons du feu," itself borrowed from the fable "Le singe et la chat," by La Fontaine. It means "to perform a difficult task on behalf of another person and without benefits from one's labor."

[Page 19]: *likouala-likouala:* The Likouala River is in the interior of the present-day Republic of Congo. By repeating the word, Césaire stresses his fascination with its sound.

[Page 20]: *voum rooh oh:* In this and the following two stanzas, Césaire evokes a shamanistic incantation. Instead of wearing the classic Western laurel, he has "on [his] black forehead a crown of daturas" (a hallucinatory plant known as jimsonweed in the United States). The "mountains uprooted at the hour when no one expects it" in the second of these three stanzas probably refers to the sudden eruption of Mount Pelée.

[Page 22]: *Torte:* a tourte in France is a crude cobbler pastry.

[Page 23]: *the Great Fear:* The end of the first millennium, A.D. 1000, was supposedly awaited with a terrible foreboding known as "The Great Fear." To "play" the game of "the millennium" would be to gamble on a total transformation of the way things are.

[Page 24]: *vitelline membrane:* the membrane protecting the egg and corresponding to the cell wall of an ordinary cell. Césaire is envisioning his own breakthrough, or self-birth, here. "The first drops of virginal milk" ten lines later which the self-born poet drinks suggests that his conception has been immaculate.

[Page 25]: *quirts:* usually a riding whip, but according to Jourdain, the word was also a popular term for a slave whip.

[Page 27]: *Gros-Morne . . . rue "De Profundis":* Gros-Morne is north of Fort-de-France. The street name here, "De Profundis," means "out of the depths" in Latin, from a liturgy for the dead.

[Page 27]: *Amazons . . . Madhis:* Amazons in this context refers to female warriors in the ancient African kingdom of Dahomey. Ghana is the medieval West African empire after which the modern nation is named. Timbuktu was an outstanding educational center in the Middle Ages. Askia the Great was ruler of Songhai (a 15th-century Malian empire). Djenné, in present-day Mali, was a university and trade center in the Middle Ages. Madhis are Islam leaders of a holy war.

[Page 28]: *chicote:* a Portuguese knotted leather slave whip.

[Page 28]: *the Calabars:* a people from southeastern Nigeria. The city of Calabar was a slave depot.

[Page 29]: *Nothing could ever lift us . . . the shape of their pelvis:* The stanza is a mishmash of physiological arguments used to describe the inferiority of the black race, notably by the French writer Arthur de Gobineau, whose theories are alluded to here. A craniometer is an instrument for measuring skull size, once thought to be a factor in the brain's evolution. "Homo sum" means "I am man," from the Latin of the Roman playwright Terence (who as a boy was the slave of a Roman senator who educated him and gave him his freedom).

[Page 30]: COMICAL AND UGLY: Césaire's phrase appears to allude to Charles Baudelaire's poem "The Albatross," where it occurs. There an albatross, once "prince of the clouds," is trapped by sailors and forced to drag its great wings about on deck.

[Page 31]: *menfenil:* According to Jourdain, the menfenil (also known as the malfini) is the *Falco sparverious caribaerum,* or the Caribbean sparrow hawk ("funereal" here not only because of the mood of the poem at this point but also because of the bird's black plumage).

[Page 32]: *chalaza:* a whip made of hard fibers.

[Page 32]: *postillion:* a household servant dressed in fine clothes whose task was to welcome the newly arrived captives and give them the impression that slaves were well treated.

[Page 35]: *Eia for the royal Cailcedra:* "Eia" is a triumphant cry; the cailcedra (a Wolof word) is the African mahogany.

[Page 37]: *to gird one's loins like a brave man:* an echo of God's words to Job: "Gird up now thy loins like a man" (Job 38:3).

[Page 38]: *wounds cut in its trunk:* probably a reference to the rubber tree, which thrives on incisions made in its trunk to produce sap.

[Page 40]: *oh those queens . . . chestnut trees:* probably refers to Césaire's memories of the Luxembourg Garden, in Paris's Latin Quarter, with its many statues of queens under chestnut tress.

[Page 40]: *the twenty-nine legal blows of the whip:* the limit prescribed by the 1865 Code Noir (Black Code) designed to regulate slave owners' treatment of their slaves. In this line, and in the twenty that follow, Césaire lists the tortures, the names of some slave holders who carried them out, and the torture devices. All of this material is documented in the writings of Victor Schoelcher (the French legislator who was most responsible for pushing the abolition laws through parliament in 1848) and are reprinted in *Esclavage et Colonisation* (Presses Universitaires de France, Paris, 1948), a collection of Schoelcher's texts, to which Césaire contributed a Preface. See in particular the chapter "La condition servile."

[Page 40]: *the fleur de lys:* The fleur de lys, or lily flower, is the emblem of the French Bourbon Dynasty, with which recaptured slaves were branded.

[Page 40]: *Mayencourt:* a slave holder who caused the death of one slave by keeping him in a dog house for six months.

[Page 44]: *the penetrance of an apocalyptic wasp:* perhaps an allusion to the plague that descended on the Egyptians before the liberation of the Israelites in Exodus 5:11.

[Page 44]: *the "lance of night" of my Bambara ancestors:* The Bamanan, known in French as Bambara, are the people of Mali. In the past, they sprinkled human blood on their spears to ensure their effectiveness in battle.

[Page 45]: *"You see . . . the sun did it":* The latter part of this speech, from "pay no attention" on, is from the Song of Solomon 1:6. These lines are paraphrased from a speech by the black Queen of Sheba, beloved of Solomon.

[Page 51]: *veerition:* According to Césaire, his "verrition" was coined off the Latin verb "verri," meaning "to sweep, to scrape a surface, to scan." Our version attempts to preserve the "veer" or turning motion (set against its oxymoronic modifier "motionless") as well as the Latin sound of the original.

A Césaire Chronology

1913 Birth of Aimé Césaire, the second of seven children, at Basse-Pointe (Martinique).

1918–24 Primary education at Basse-Pointe.

1924 Secondary education at the Lycée Schoelcher in Fort-de-France. Meets Léon Damas.

1932 Obtains his *baccalauréat* with such distinction that he is awarded a scholarship to continue his education in France. Arrives in France and is admitted to the Lycée Louis-le-Grand, where he enrolls in the preparatory class for the entrance exam to the prestigious Ecole Normale Supérieure. Meets Léopold Sédar Senghor (who is seven years his senior).

1935 Participates in the creation of *L'Etudiant Noir* and gains admission to the Ecole Normale Supérieure.

1936 Begins to compose *Cahier d'un retour au pays natal* during a trip to Yugoslavia (and visiting with his friend Petar Guberina the island of Martinska in the Adriatic Sea).

1937 Marries Suzanne Roussi; completes the *Cahier*.

1939 Publication of the *Cahier* in *Volontés* magazine. Césaire returns to Martinique with his family.

1940 Becomes a teacher of French and classical literatures at his old lycée in Fort-de-France (among his students were Edouard Glissant and Georges Desportes). With René Ménil, and his wife, Suzanne, creates the literary review *Tropiques* (1941–45).

1941 André Breton, on his way to voluntary exile in the United States, visits Martinique and meets the Césaires.

1944 Césaire spends seven months in Haiti; in September, gives a keynote address, entitled "Poetry and Knowledge," at a conference on philosophy in Port-au-Prince.

1945 Césaire is elected mayor of Fort-de-France and, as a member of the French Communist Party, one of the deputies for Martinique to the Constituent Assembly in Paris.

1946 Publication of *Les armes miraculeuses* (The Miraculous Weapons).

1947 Césaire is one of a group of writers who support Alioune Diop in the founding of Présence Africaine, in Paris.

1948 Jean-Paul Sartre publishes "Orphée noir," offering an extended formulation to the concept of *négritude,* in Senghor's *Anthologie de la nouvelle poésie nègre et malgache.* Césaire publishes *Soleil cou coupé* (Solar Throat Slashed).

1949 Publication of *Corps perdu* (Lost Body), with thirty-two engravings by Pablo Picasso.

1950 Publication of the long polemic *Discours sur le colonialisme* (Discourse on Colonialism).

1956 Delivers the address, "Culture et Colonisation" at the Premier Congrès de Ecrivains Noirs organized by Présence Africaine. Breaks with the Communist Party.

1958 Founds his own party, the Parti Progressiste Martiniquais. Theatrical performance of Césaire's oratorio *Et les chiens se taisaient* (And the Dogs Were Silent).

1960 Publication of *Ferrements* (Ferraments).

1961 Publication of *Cadastre* (comprised of a reedited *Soleil cou coupé* and *Corps perdu*).

1962 Publication of a historical study of the Haitian revolution, *Toussaint Louverture, ou la révolution française et le problème colonial* (Toussaint L'Ouverture, or the French Revolution and the Colonial Problem).

1963 Publication of *La Tragédie du Roi Christophe* (a play).

1967 Publication of *Une Saison au Congo* (a play).

1969 Publication of *Une Tempête* (a play).

1976 Publication of the *Oeuvres Complètes* (three volumes).

1982 Publication of *moi, laminaire* (i, laminaria).

1994 Publication of *Aimé Césaire: La Poésie* (ed. by Daniel Maximin and Gilles Carpentier).

2001 Césaire continues to live in Fort-de-France and is completing his last term as mayor of the city.

ABOUT THE AUTHOR

AIMÉ CÉSAIRE is perhaps best known as the co-creator (with Léopold Senghor) of the concept of *négritude*. A former member of the Communist Party and active supporter of a progressive Socialist movement in his native Martinique, he has a profuse intellectual knowledge of European literature and history, as well as a passion for promoting Black culture and studies. Through a unique combination of Black subjectivity and European Surrealism that causes his work to possess an exotic and unmatched style, his poetry describes the colonized condition of Caribbean, African, and Third World peoples, while also addressing "universal hunger, universal thirst." Césaire's *Notebook of a Return to the Native Land* was first published in 1947. His complete poetry, entitled *La Poésie*, was published by Editions du Seuil, Paris, 1994.

ABOUT THE TRANSLATORS/EDITORS

CLAYTON ESHLEMAN has published twelve books of poetry and has translated works by Antonin Artaud, Bernard Bador, Michel Deguy, Vladimir Holan, Pablo Neruda, and César Vallejo. He is a professor of English at Eastern Michigan University.

ANNETTE SMITH is an Emeritus Professor of Literature at the California Institute of Technology. Besides publishing books and articles on various aspects of colonialism and racism, she has co-authored with Clayton Eshleman three previous translations of Aimé Césaire, one of which, *Aimé Césaire: The Collected Poetry* (1983), won the Witter Bynner Award from the Poetry Society of America.

Library of Congress Cataloging-in-Publication Data

Césaire, Aimé.
[Cahier d'un retour au pays natal. English]
Notebook of a return to the native land / Aimé Césaire ; translated
and edited by Clayton Eshleman and Annette Smith.
p. cm. — (Wesleyan poetry)
ISBN 0-8195-6452-4
I. Eshleman, Clayton. II. Smith, Annette. III. Title. IV. Series.
PQ2605.E74 C313 2001
841'.914—dc21   2001000114